christmas carols

Very Easy Piano

Arranged by Heather Milnes

Copyright © 2016 by Heather Milnes
First published in the U.K. in 2016 by
The Ashton Book Company
9 Dairy Farm, Ashton Keynes,
Swindon, Wiltshire SN6 6NZ
All rights reserved

ISBN-13: 978-1539845577
ISBN-10: 1539845575

CONTENTS

Away in a Manger	5
Andrew Mine, Jasper Mine	6
I Saw Three Ships	7
The First Nowell	8
Jingle Bells	9
Silent Night	10
While Shepherds Watched	11
We Three Kings	12
Good King Wenceslas	14
Once in Royal David's City	15
In the Bleak Mid-Winter	16
Jolly Old Saint Nicholas	17
See Amid the Winter's Snow	18
O Little Town of Bethlehem	19
O Come All Ye Faithful	20
The Holly and the Ivy	21
Sans Day Carol	22
Deck the Hall	23
Hark the Herald Angels Sing	24
We Wish You a Merry Christmas	25

AWAY IN A MANGER

Slowly and gently

W. J. Kirkpatrick

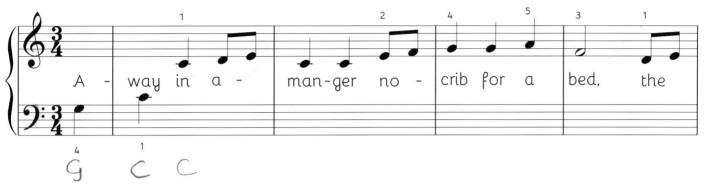

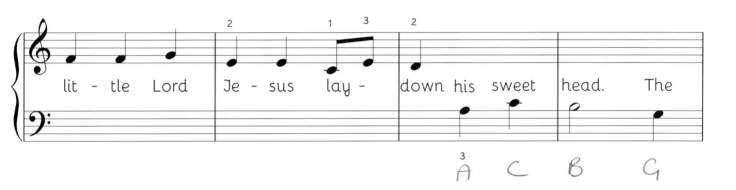

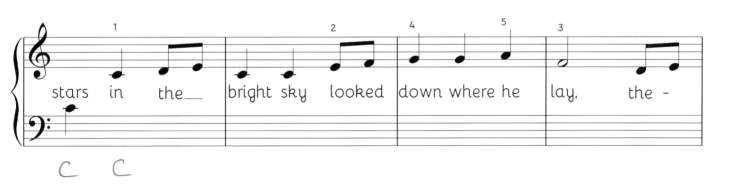

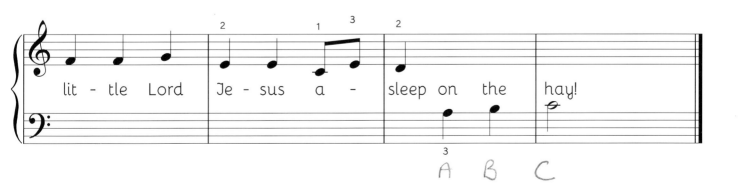

ANDREW MINE, JASPER MINE

At a medium pace

Traditional Moravian carol

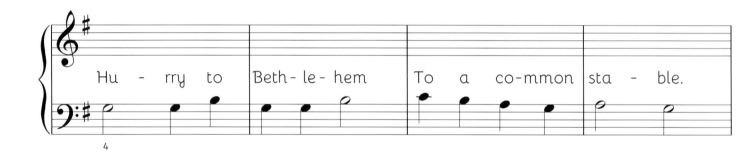

I SAW THREE SHIPS

Lively

English traditional carol

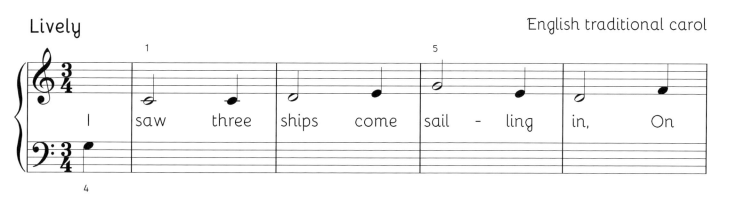
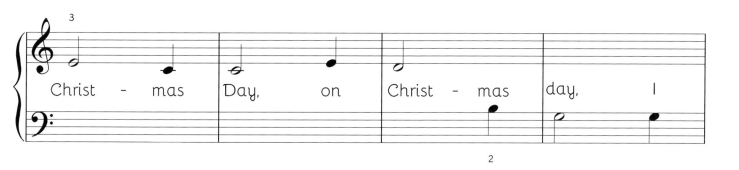

THE FIRST NOWELL

Happy!

English traditional carol

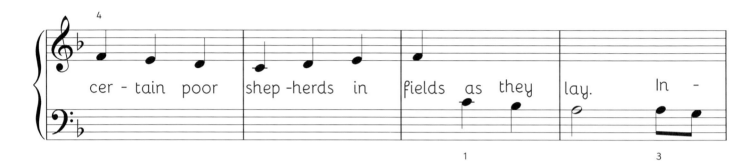
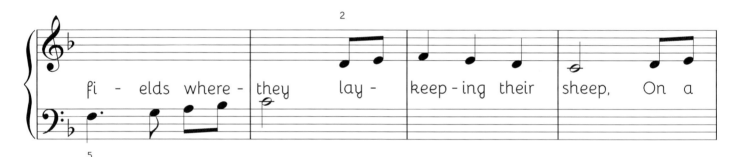
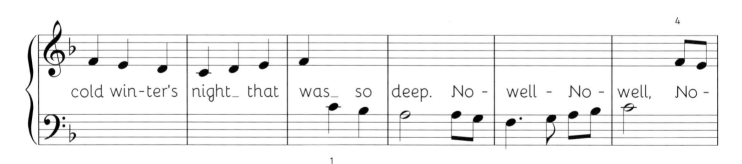
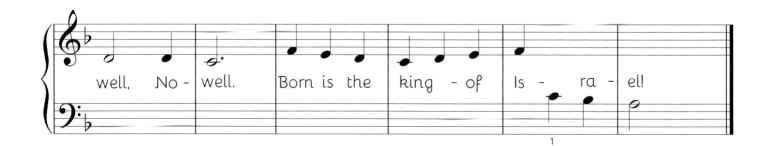

JINGLE BELLS

Quick and lively

James Pierpont

Jin - gle Bells, Jin - gle Bells, Jin - gle all the way,

Oh what fun it is to ride in a one horse o - pen sleigh Hey

Jin - gle Bells, Jin - gle Bells, Jin - gle all the way,

Oh what fun it is to ride in a one horse o - pen sleigh!

SILENT NIGHT

Peacefully

Franz Gruber

Si – lent night, ho – ly night.

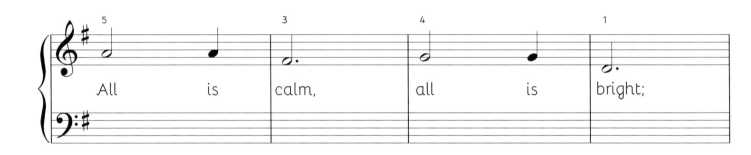

All is calm, all is bright;

round yon Vir – gin Moth – er and child

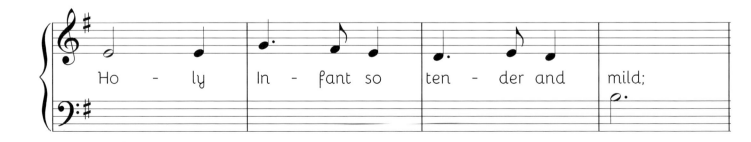

Ho – ly In – fant so ten – der and mild;

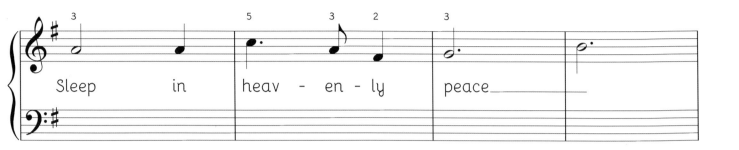

Sleep in heav – en – ly peace_____

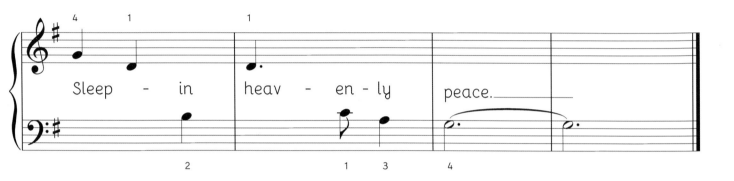

Sleep – in heav – en – ly peace._____

WHILE SHEPHERDS WATCHED

Traditional English carol

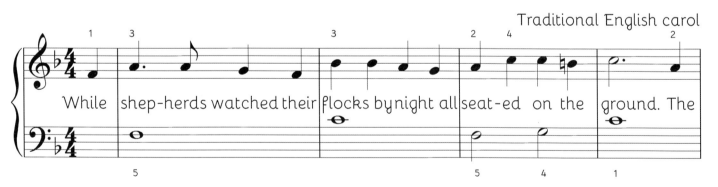

While shep-herds watched their flocks by night all seat-ed on the ground. The

an – gel of the Lord came down, And glo – ry shone a – round.

WE THREE KINGS

With movement

J. H. Hopkins

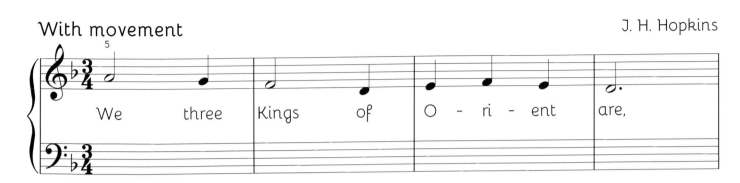

We three Kings of O - ri - ent are,

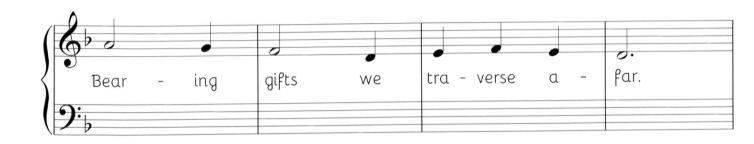

Bear - ing gifts we tra - verse a - far.

Field and foun - tain, moor and moun__ tain

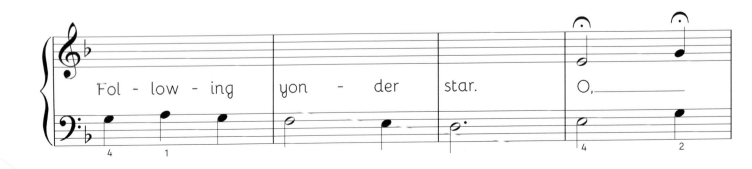

Fol - low - ing yon - der star. O,_____

Star of won - der, star of night,

Star with ro - yal beau - ty bright.

West - ward lead - ing still pro - ceed - ing,

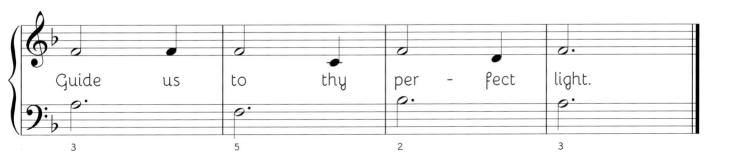

Guide us to thy per - fect light.

GOOD KING WENCESLAS

Lively

Old English melody

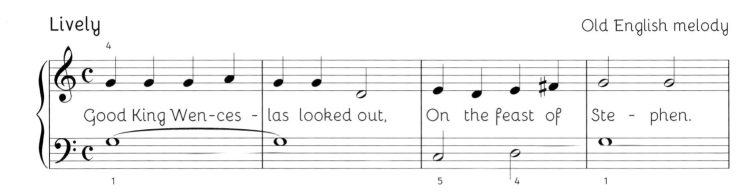

Good King Wen-ces - las looked out, On the feast of Ste - phen.

When the snow lay round a -bout, deep and crisp and e - ven.

Bright-ly shone the moon that night, Though the frost was cru - el,

When a poor man came in sight, Gath'-ring win -ter fu_____ el.

ONCE IN ROYAL DAVID'S CITY

English

Majestically

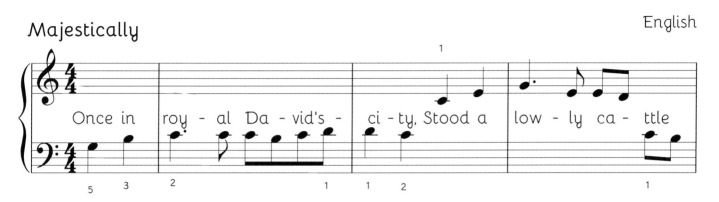

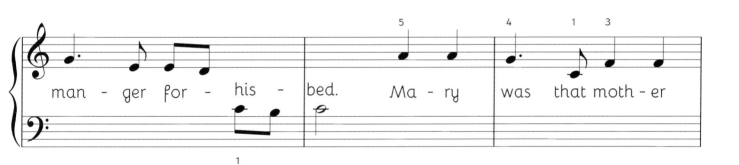

IN THE BLEAK MID-WINTER

Lively

Gustav Holst

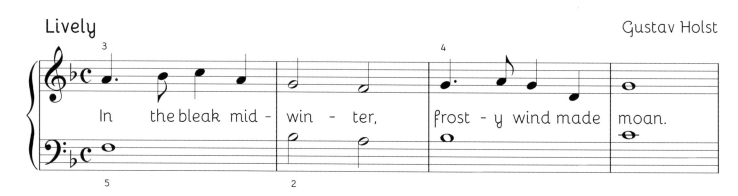

In the bleak mid - win - ter, frost - y wind made moan.

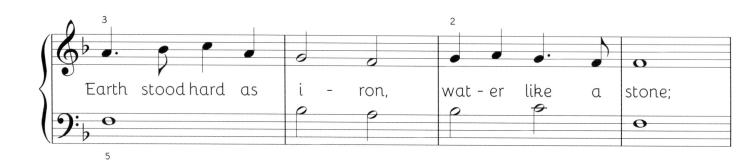

Earth stood hard as i - ron, wat-er like a stone;

Snow had fal -len, snow on snow, snow - on - snow.

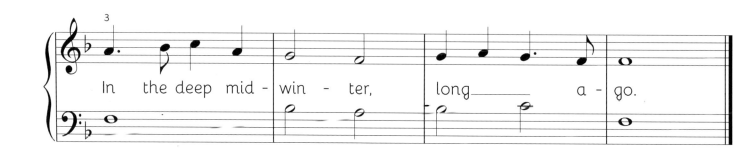

In the deep mid - win - ter, long_____ a - go.

JOLLY OLD SAINT NICHOLAS

American

Allegro

Jol - ly old Saint Nich - o - las, Lend your ear this way,

Don't you tell a sin - gle soul What I'm going to say;

Christ-mas Eve is com-ing soon, Now, you dear old man,

Whis-per what you'll bring to me, Tell me if you can.

SEE AMID THE WINTER'S SNOW

Moderato

Traditional English carol

O LITTLE TOWN OF BETHLEHEM

Traditional English carol

Andante

O li - ttle town of Beth_ le - hem how still we_ see thee lie! A-

bove thy deep and dream less sleep the si lent stars go by. Yet_

in thy dark streets shin_____ neth the e - ve last-ting light. The

hopes and fears of all - our - years are met in - thee to night.

O COME ALL YE FAITHFUL

Con moto

J. F. Wade

THE HOLLY AND THE IVY

Vivo

Traditional English carol

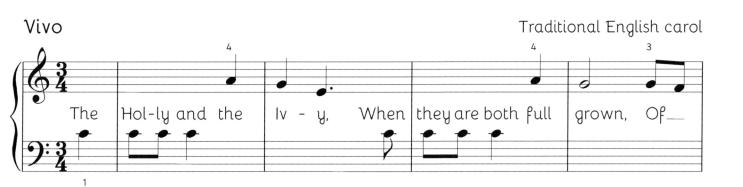

The Hol-ly and the Iv - y, When they are both full grown, Of__

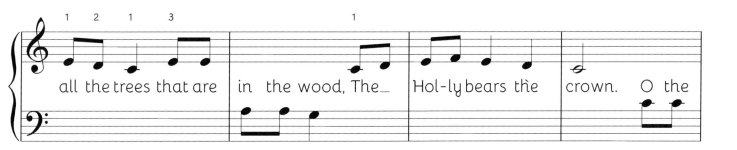

all the trees that are in the wood, The__ Hol-ly bears the crown. O the

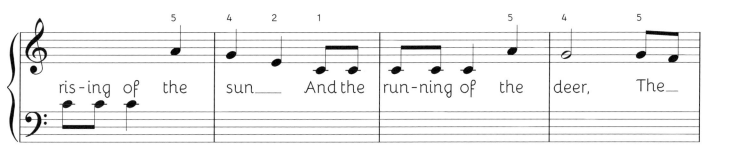

ris-ing of the sun__ And the run-ning of the deer, The__

play-ing of the me-rry or -gan, Sweet sing-ing in the choir.

SANS DAY CAROL

Allegretto

Traditional Cornish carol

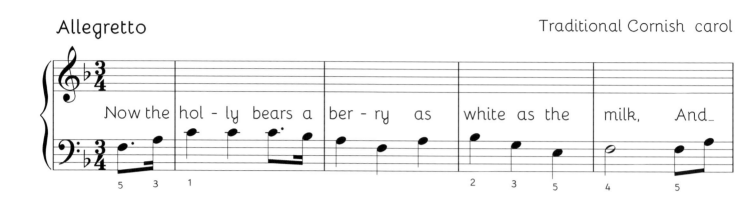

Now the hol – ly bears a ber – ry as white as the milk, And

Ma – ry bore Je – sus all wrapped up in silk: And

Ma – ry bore Je-sus Christ our Sav –iour for to be, And the

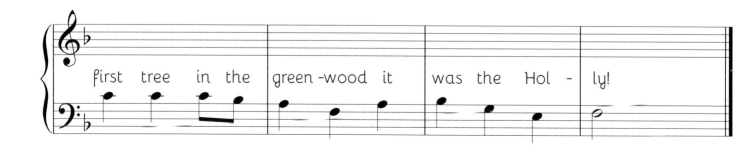

first tree in the green -wood it was the Hol – ly!

DECK THE HALL

Welsh traditional carol

Vivace

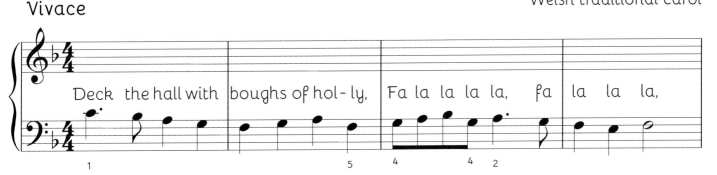

Deck the hall with boughs of hol-ly, Fa la la la la, fa la la la,

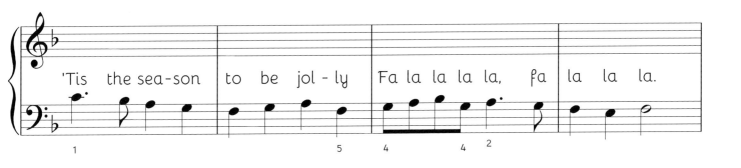

'Tis the sea-son to be jol-ly Fa la la la la, fa la la la.

Fill the mead cup, drain the bar-rel, Fa la la, fa la la, la la la,

Troll the an-cient Christ-mas car-ol, Fa la la la la, fa la la la.

HARK THE HERALD ANGELS SING

Maestoso

F. Mendelssohn

WE WISH YOU A MERRY CHRISTMAS

Traditional west country carol

Allegro

We wish you a Mer-ry Christ -mas, we wish you a Mer-ry Christ -mas, we

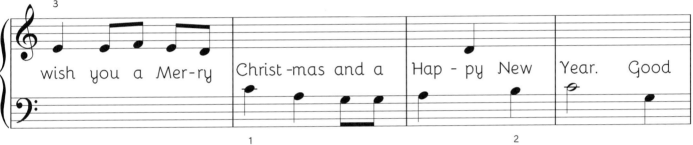

wish you a Mer-ry Christ -mas and a Hap - py New Year. Good

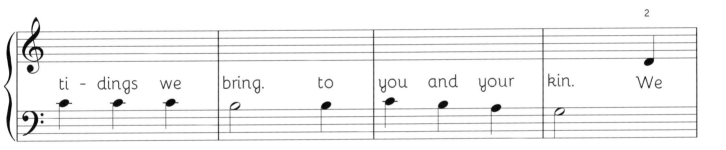

ti - dings we bring. to you and your kin. We

wish you a Mer-ry Christ mas and a Hap - py New Year.

Merry Christmas

Printed in Poland
by Amazon Fulfillment
Poland Sp. z o.o., Wrocław

65839801R00016